Albert Einstein

Physicist and Genius

GREAT MINDS OF SCIENCE

Albert Einstein
Physicist and Genius

Joyce Goldenstern

Enslow Publishers, Inc.

40 Industrial Road
Box 398
Berkeley Heights, NJ 07922
USA

PO Box 38
Aldershot
Hants GU12 6BP
UK

http://www.enslow.com

For family members and friends who have listened patiently to my ravings about light, space, time, and the one unifying force.

Library of Congress Cataloging-In-Publication Data

Goldenstern, Joyce.
    Albert Einstein: Physicist and genius / by Joyce Goldenstern.
        p. cm. — (Great minds of science)
    Includes bibliographical references and index.
    ISBN 0-7660-1864-4 (pbk)
    ISBN 0-89490-480-9 (library ed.)
    1. Einstein, Albert, 1879–1955—Biography—Juvenile literature.
    2. Physicists—Biography—Juvenile literature. [1. Einstein,
    Albert, 1879–1955. 2. Physicists.] I. Title. II. Series.
    QC16.E5G65   1995
    530.092—dc20
    [B]   94-860
                                                           CIP
                                                           AC

Printed in the United States of America

10 9 8 7

To Our Readers:
All Internet Addresses in this book were active and appropriate when we
went to press. Any comments or suggestions can be sent by e-mail to
Comments@enslow.com or to the address on the back cover.

Photo Credits: Art Institute of Chicago, p. 68; California Institute of Technology Archives, Photo Collection, p. 103; F.D.R. Library, p. 93; German Information Center, pp. 71, 100; The Hebrew University of Jerusalem, pp. 24, 37, 53; Inter Nationes, pp. 18, 22, 28; Library of Congress, pp. 9, 15, 40, 47, 77; National Archives, pp. 87, 94, 106; Swiss National Tourist Office, pp. 33, 44, 56; The Time Museum, Rockford, Illinois, p. 64.

Illustration Credits: Kim Austin, pp. 20, 45, 76, 79, 81, 109.

Cover Photo Credits: U.S. Naval Observatory Photo (background); Library of Congress (inset).

Contents

1 A Daring New Look 7

2 Captivated by a Compass 17

3 View from the
Office Window 32

4 Photons of Light
Dancing in His Head 46

5 Trains Zipping By 55

6 Freely Falling in Space 70

7 The Conscience
of a Scientist   83

8 In the Temple of Science . . .   96

Activities   108

Chronology   115

Notes by Chapter   117

Glossary   121

Further Reading   125

Internet Addresses   125

Index   126

1

A Daring New Look

THE YEAR: 1950. THE PLACE: PRINCETON, New Jersey. Princeton is a town of tradition. Here, in 1776, American colonials fought a battle for independence. Here, in 1783, the Continental Congress met. And in that same year, General George Washington delivered his "Farewell Address to the Armies." In the town cemetery a visitor easily finds graves marked with famous names—such as Aaron Burr and Grover Cleveland.

But the Princeton of 1950 thought more of the future than of the past; more of life than of death. World War II was over. Citizens looked forward to good times. The Princeton University campus bustled with young people who looked ahead.

Two men walked together through the campus every day. One was not young; he was an old man. He had amazing long white hair that stuck up every which way. A shaggy moustache drooped over his mouth. He often wore baggy pants. And he usually smoked a battered old pipe. He had kind, deep brown eyes, but a few strange habits. For example, he seldom wore socks. In the morning he would quickly lace up his shoes without putting any on. He had no time to bother with socks!

Students sometimes turned their heads as the two men passed. Some of them recognized the old man. He was the famous scientist Albert Einstein. In 1950 he was seventy-one years old. He had been ill; stomach pains would sometimes get the better of him. Many of the people he loved were dead. In spite of his age and sorrows, Einstein was not out of place on a college campus. Like the young people around him, he thought more of the future than of the past. More of life than of

Albert Einstein lived from 1879 to 1955. He spent his later years in Princeton, New Jersey.

death. He lived for his quest. Before he died, he wanted to find one physical force that unifies all natural forces.

Einstein walked home nearly every day with his young friend Abraham Pais. Both men were scientists. Both men worked at the Institute for Advanced Study. Actually, Einstein had retired several years previously. Still he often went to his office at the Institute.

Abraham Pais knew he had much to learn from Einstein. One day, he paid Einstein a visit in his office. He wanted to better understand Einstein's ideas. Some of them he just could not get a hold on. Einstein suggested that they walk while they talked. And so they did, almost every day. Einstein talked slowly, but with great passion.

All of his life, Einstein had enjoyed long walks. He walked and talked as he courted his first wife Mileva. (Mileva, like Einstein, studied to be a scientist.) He walked and talked with their friend Marcel Grossman at the Federal Polytechnic Academy. All three young people studied there.

Later, he drank tea and ate sausages on

country outings with Maurice Solovine and Conrad Habicht. Einstein tutored these two young men. The three of them formed a club called the Olympia Academy. Philosophy and science thrilled them. They took long walks together and talked for hours about thoughts that have troubled humans for centuries: What is knowledge? What is truth? What is the purpose of science? Einstein loved to ask tough questions.

"Do you believe," Einstein asked Abraham Pais one day, "that the moon exists only if you look at it? What does 'to exist' mean, anyway? I mean what does it mean to exist when you talk about inanimate objects?"[1]

Albert Einstein often asked Pais such questions. Nature always made him wonder. Walking with a friend allowed his imagination to roam. The questions about the moon remained unanswered, but no matter. The questions themselves were important to Einstein. Curiosity and wonder filled his days.

Almost everyone has heard of Albert Einstein. Advertisers use his name or image to make a point. An ad for an electric company has a drawing of Albert Einstein. The caption reads, "You don't have to be a nuclear physicist to understand an electric bill." In other words, "You don't have to be an Einstein!"

"Einstein" is not just the last name of Albert Einstein. It has become a common noun. "Einstein" means genius.

But Einstein did not consider himself to be a genius. Someone once asked him where he got his intelligence—from his mother or his father? Einstein explained that curiosity helped him to form important theories. Curiosity was more important for him than intelligence.

Of course, Einstein had to understand hard concepts. He had to know a lot of math and physics to come up with his theories. But Einstein never whizzed through his studies as a student. He knew how trying math problems could be.[2]

When he was at Princeton, young people wrote him letters. They asked him to explain tough problems. They told him about their troubles with science and math. One twelve-year-old student complained that mathematics confused her. Einstein wrote, "Do not worry about your difficulties in mathematics. I can assure you that mine are still greater."[3]

Einstein did have a hard time in school. So why do we call him a genius? We sometimes think intelligence means being quick to solve school problems. But Einstein plodded through school. He preferred to follow his own interests. He studied at his own slow rate. His thoughts often wandered.

He decided for himself what mysteries of nature to study. He did not become confused by the many special areas of study. He did not become weighted down. He asked basic questions: What is light? What is time? What is mass? What is energy? What is acceleration? What is gravity? He took nothing for granted.

The ideas of the famous scientist Isaac Newton had served people well for centuries. They led to inventions such as the steam engine and the telegraph. For most scientists these old ideas worked well enough, but at the turn of the century certain problems puzzled other scientists. During the 1800s, scientists learned more about magnets and about electricity. They learned more about optics, which is the science of light. Also engineers crafted better measuring tools. Soon scientists realized that Newton's theories did not always work. For example, scientists could not perfectly chart the orbit of the planet Mercury using Newton's laws.

There is an old story about three blind men and an elephant. Each blind man stands close to the elephant. Each touches a particular part of its body. One man touches the elephant's ear. He thinks the elephant is thin and shaped like a saucer. Another man touches the elephant's trunk. He imagines the elephant is long and shaped like a hose. A third touches the elephant's leg. He supposes the elephant is thick and shaped like a column.

What should the blind men do to understand what an elephant really looks like? They need to feel the entire elephant, of course. A sighted

Albert Einstein stands with his second wife, Elsa, in front of their Princeton home.

person only has to take a step back and look at the whole animal.

The point of that old tale is that sometimes we get stuck in one place. We keep inspecting a problem in one way. So we do not see clearly. We need enough sense to step back.

Albert Einstein respected the ideas of Isaac Newton. But Einstein was willing to take a new look. When he did, he suddenly saw vexing problems with new insight. So he helped science move ahead. In upcoming chapters you will learn more about Einstein's vision. Why is he considered a genius? Partly because he dared to take a new look.

Captivated by a Compass

DRUMS ROLLED, FIFES SOUNDED THEIR NOTES, windows rattled, the ground shook, and splendid horses pranced to the rhythms. These were the sounds and sights of a military parade. In the 1800s, Germany celebrated holidays with military parades. The colorful parades drew children to them as though by magic. Just like the Pied Piper, the soldiers cast a binding spell. The children marched behind them. The youngsters tried hard to keep in step. Their small palms beat imaginary drums. Their tiny fingers danced in the air just like the fingers of fife players! Their shoulders bore the weight of invisible rifles.

Kaiser Wilhelm I (left) and Otto von Bismarck (right) united all regions of Germany under Prussian rule.

"When you grow up, you can be a soldier!" German parents often said to their delighted sons.

"When I grow up, I don't want to be one of those poor people," Albert Einstein cried.[1] He stood with his parents in Munich, Germany. He sadly watched the sight. Tears rolled down his cheeks. To him it was like a nightmare. He hated the mechanical motion. He hated the uniforms. And he hated the lack of freedom.

During the 1880s, Germany grew mighty. The Franco-Prussian War had just ended. The great Prussian military leader Otto von Bismarck united all the regions of Germany. Prussia was the most powerful region of Germany. It was known for its military strength. By the 1880s, Bismarck and the Prussian army ruled Germany with "iron and blood." In other words, they ruled with a tight fist. Bismarck rejoiced in military and industrial power. His soldiers marched throughout the country.

Albert's ancestors had not lived in Prussia. The Einstein family had come from the Swabia region

1879

North Sea · DENMARK · Baltic Sea · NETH. · BELGIUM · PRUSSIA · Berlin · RUSSIAN EMPIRE · FRANCE · GERMANY · Aarau · Zurich · Ulm · Munich · Bern · SWITZERLAND · AUSTRIA-HUNGARY · ITALY · SERBIA · ROMANIA · MONTENEGRO · BULGARIA · OTTOMAN EMPIRE · GREECE · Mediterranean Sea

Albert Einstein was born in Germany during a time of its military growth. Prussia was the strongest German state. Later Einstein moved to Switzerland.

in the southwest. So had the Koch family, the family of Albert's mother. Swabia was a quiet region of Germany. People there kept shops and made shoes. They crafted silverware and traded goods. They also enjoyed reading the Bible and *Tales of the Black Forest.*

Albert Einstein was born in Ulm, Germany, on March 14, 1879. Within a year, though, his parents moved to Munich, Germany. There, at a young age, Albert often saw military parades. Even if he wished to ignore them, he could not. The noise rushed through the streets of Munich. It caught up everyone in its path.

Noise and military displays did not interest little Albert. He was a quiet child. Indeed, he did not learn to speak until he was three years old. Even then, he did not speak very well. At nine, he still stumbled over his words. Other boys played soldier and fought. But young Albert did not join in. Maja, his sister, became his best friend. She was his only sister, born two years after him; he had no brothers. Often he played alone. He enjoyed building houses out of cards. He practiced the violin. And sometimes he just stared into space. At times, his teachers made fun of his solitary ways. They called him "Father Bore."

Hermann Einstein and his wife Pauline cared for their children with patience. They loved their

Albert Einstein grew up in Munich, Germany, a beautiful city in the heart of the region called Bavaria. Its parks and squares are filled with elegant fountains and sculptures.

son, even though he was different from most children. "Maybe he'll be a professor," Pauline used to say. Pauline played the piano. She taught her children to love classical music. Hermann laughed a lot. He loved to surprise his children with presents.

One day, he brought home a compass for five-year-old Albert. Albert was sick in bed. So Hermann wanted to cheer him. Albert Einstein always treasured that gift. It changed his life. The compass captivated him. He moved the compass every which way. But its needle always pointed north. Why? Albert wondered.[2] What invisible force drove the needle? Another amazing thing was that the needle seemed to float. What held it up? These questions filled his mind. Years later he wrote about the compass, "I can still remember—or at least believe I can remember— that this experience made a deep and lasting impression on me. Something deeply hidden had to be behind things."[3]

Something hidden behind things? He wanted to understand what it was. The order of military

Albert Einstein with his sister, Maja.

parades scared him. But the order of the universe thrilled him. The mystery of the pocket compass stayed with him for a long time. When he was older, he learned more about magnets. He then knew that the earth's magnetic field made the needle point to the north.

His parents sent Albert to a Catholic grade school because it was nearby. Albert enjoyed studying the Catholic religion. He thought that religion might help him understand the mysteries of nature.

But Albert was the only Jew in the school. The other children began to tease him because he was Jewish. In the 1870s, a man named Wilhelm Marr had founded the League of Anti-Semites. Anti-Semites blamed Jewish people for money problems in Germany. So some German children felt it was okay to make fun of Jews. Albert hated the prejudice.[4]

Albert's parents did not attend synagogue. They did, however, keep some nonreligious customs. For example, they invited a poor person to share dinner with them once a week. Most Jews did this. The Einsteins always invited Max Talmey, a medical student. Remembering these days, Maja once wrote, "Our family was very close-knit and very hospitable."[5]

Soon Max and Albert became friends. Max began to bring books to show Albert. These included *Force and Matter* by L. Buchner and *Popular Books of Physical Science* by A. Bernstein. Albert read these books with zest. Before long, he turned from religion to science in his search to understand nature.

His search led him to investigate mathematics too. Albert's uncle Jacob Einstein was an engineer. He introduced Albert to algebra. Algebra is a part of mathematics used to find an unknown quantity. In algebra the letter "X" often stands for the unknown number. "Algebra is a merry science," Uncle Jacob told Albert. "When the animal that we are hunting cannot be caught, we call it X temporarily and continue to hunt it until it is bagged."[6]

Jacob also taught Albert geometry. Geometry is another part of mathematics. It deals with lines, points, and angles. Albert loved hearing about geometry. It seemed "lucid and certain," he later said.[7]

Albert sometimes stumbled over calculations. He made mistakes in addition and subtraction. But he began to understand advanced concepts of algebra and geometry. His deep interest amazed both Jacob and Max.

School, though, was another story. There he amazed almost no one. After finishing grade school, Albert attended the Luitpold Gymnasium. A gymnasium in Germany is a high school. Albert hated the school. Some of his teachers complained that he always looked very bored. Others scolded him for asking too many questions. He said, "The teachers in the elementary school appeared to me like sergeants, and the gymnasium teachers like lieutenants."[8]

In the meantime Bismarck's control continued to spread—in the schools, on the street, in businesses, and in industries. Industry in the Germany of the 1880s flourished. Monopolies flexed their muscles.[9] Monopolies are huge

Otto von Bismarck ruled with "iron and blood." Einstein hated the military spirit. But it spread throughout Germany.

companies that often buy out smaller businesses. The main monopolies in Germany in the 1880s manufactured chemical and electrical products.

Hermann Einstein ran an electrical factory. Together with his brother Jacob, he manufactured dynamos, electric instruments, and arc lights. But theirs was a small factory. Soon they found that they could not compete with giant monopolies such as Siemens & Halske. Siemens & Halske had improved telegraphs. It dominated the electrical industry. Eventually, Hermann's factory failed. He had to look for a new job.

His father had not been very lucky with electricity. But Albert loved learning about it. All around him, people spoke of cables and telegraphs. The use of batteries, coils, electric lights, railways, and power plants was spreading across the world. People dreamed of telephones and radios and aurophones for deafness. They also imagined more exotic inventions such as electric cigarettes, garters, and curling combs. Einstein got caught up in the excitement. He began to read about the discoveries that had led up to the age of electricity.

In 1894, Hermann moved the family to Italy in order to start a new business. Albert was fifteen then. He was supposed to stay behind in Germany and finish up his studies. But Albert soon quit school and headed for Italy. He was happy to leave the strict school. Also, he hoped to avoid the German military draft. He was determined to give up his German citizenship. Later he did so.

After a while, Hermann sent him to school in Switzerland. He wanted Albert to study at the Federal Polytechnic Academy in Zurich. Unfortunately, Albert failed to pass the entrance exam. The director of the Academy told him that he could enter after a while. But first, he must prepare at another school in Aarau, Switzerland.

Albert liked one of his teachers in Aarau. His name was August Tuschmid. He spoke to Albert Einstein about the central problem in physics. The central problem in physics had to do with Newton's mechanical view of the universe. Scientists had been using Isaac Newton's ideas for nearly three hundred years. During that time scientists learned more about magnetism and electricity. They realized they were the same force. They called it electromagnetism. But how were Newton's laws and electromagnetism related? This was physics' central problem— bringing these two ideas together. The greatest minds in Europe were at work on the problem. Albert longed to come up with the answer.

View from the Office Window

EACH TIME THE CLOCK STRIKES THE hour, wooden bears dance and a toy knight draws his sword. This clock, housed in a huge tower, graces the city of Bern, Switzerland. The whimsical timepiece can be seen from many windows. Citizens who stroll in the surrounding square admire it. Children who sit by the city's fountains raise their faces. They wait eagerly for the bears to dance.

One can easily imagine Albert Einstein looking out from his office window. Perhaps he was there early in the morning before the other

The famous clock tower in Bern, Switzerland, can be seen from many windows of the city. Einstein lived in Bern from 1902 to 1909.

workers. As he stared at the clock, did he think about time? Perhaps he did. For it was in Bern that Einstein formed his theory about time.

From the years 1902 to 1909, Einstein lived in Bern and worked at the Swiss Patent Office. He worked as a civil servant, even though he had studied to be a teacher. Albert had enjoyed studying the theories of physics at the Federal Polytechnic Academy. But when Albert graduated, he could not find a steady teaching job. He wandered from one job to the next. Finally his friend Marcel Grossman found a civil service job for Albert.

Albert Einstein liked his job in the Swiss Patent Office. He had to write up reports on patent applications. Patents are registrations for new inventions. All the new inventions around him at work amused Einstein. He also enjoyed the company of his office mates. After work, Einstein walked home with Michaelangelo Besso. Einstein explained to Besso his ideas about time and light. Besso listened thoughtfully. "If they are roses, they will bloom," he said to Einstein about his ideas.[1]

Einstein's boss at the patent office was a strict, but kind man. His name was Friedrich Haller. He insisted that his employees write their reports perfectly. Einstein did not mind. At the Swiss Patent Office, Albert Einstein became a very clear writer. This skill later helped him explain his complex ideas. He could explain them to other scientists as well as to ordinary people.

Sometimes Einstein came early to the office to work on his own theories. Perhaps he arrived early to also get away from problems at home. He and his wife Mileva no longer got along. They had married in 1903 after a long courtship. Mileva was an intelligent woman. She had studied with Einstein at the Polytechnic Academy. As young students they became very close. They discussed scientific ideas with vigor. Some people believe that Mileva helped Einstein form his theories.[2] "I'm so lucky to have found you," Einstein wrote to her in a letter when they were students. "A creature who is my equal, and who is strong and independent as I am! I feel alone with everyone except you."[3]

With time, though, their love soured. Before they married, they had had a child. They named the little girl Lieserl. Since Albert could not find a job then, the young couple could not marry. Mileva bore the child alone. After a while, she gave her up for adoption. Perhaps the great sorrow of losing a child made Mileva bitter.

Also, Mileva did not adjust well to Albert's idea of marriage. She might have preferred being a full-time scientist to keeping house. Albert expected a wife to keep house. That way he would have time to study. Mileva had little time to read or discuss scientific ideas. Soon after they married, the couple had two more children. First Hans Albert, then Eduard. Mileva spent her days cooking and cleaning. She took care of the little boys.

Einstein loved his children and helped to care for them. But he did not like to deal with personal life. He escaped in his work. The laws of nature captured almost all of his attention.

Mileva, the first wife of Albert Einstein, with their sons Eduard (left) and Hans Albert (right).

When alone, Einstein still thought a lot about unifying the mechanical view of the universe with electromagnetism. Bringing the two together was still the central problem of physics. During his days at the office, Einstein puzzled over these two views. Let us take a look at them too. They will help us understand the science of Albert Einstein.

Long ago, people assumed that the sun revolved around the earth. They believed that the earth was the center of the universe. They also believed in a final purpose for all things. For example, when they saw light shining through a lantern, they said it shone so that people would not stumble in the dark. Or when people heard thunder, they said it was loud in order to scare people into being good. In other words, they believed that nonliving things served a purpose for people.

This idea of final purpose could not be proved very well by logic. Nor could it be proved by observation. But it made people feel important. Then, in 1543, Copernicus announced a new idea. Actually, it was a forgotten idea, not a new one. He claimed that the earth moves around the sun, the sun does not move around the earth. This upset many people. This made them think that maybe people on earth were no longer the center of the universe. Perhaps everything was not created for people's benefit. The work of scientists shifted. Scientists began to describe events in terms of what they observed. They no longer talked about final purpose very much.

In the early 1600s, Galileo had proposed an experiment. He wanted to drop two objects together. He believed that a heavy brick and a light feather would land at the same time. Well, the air might cause the feather to float a bit longer. But take air away, and the two objects would fall together. Though he probably never performed the experiment, his ideas were later proved correct.

In 1666, Sir Isaac Newton built upon the ideas of Galileo. He applied mathematics to nature. Using his studies he set down laws of motion and gravity. In science, laws are explanations of natural forces that always seem to be true.

Newton's calculations showed that objects in the universe such as moons, stars, and planets are attracted to each other. The strength of the attraction depends on the mass of the objects. On earth, mass is equal to weight. The attraction also depends on the distance between the objects. Newton measured the distance using straight lines.

Newton calculated the relation between mass

and distance. He called this relation the law of gravity. The law of gravity seemed to be true for many physical events. It accurately described the way the moon went around the earth, the way the earth revolved around the sun, and the way objects fell to the earth. The fall of the apple in a

Isaac Newton (1642–1727) was the first to describe the law of gravity. Great advances in science were made based on his ideas.

legend about Newton can be described by this law too. In the legend, an apple fell from a tree and hit Newton on the head. The knock on the head helped him to understand the law of gravity. Newton's law explained nature in a simple way. His view came to be called mechanics.

Scientists later found that the mechanical view also described gasses. They liked to think that the mechanical view could explain almost everything. Scientists of the 1700s and 1800s often thought of the universe as a huge machine. All of the movements of the machine could be predicted using the mechanical view of Newton.

Soon scientists were stuck in this rut. They couldn't see beyond Newton's laws. Some physical events could not be described very well using Newton's laws. But scientists tended to ignore this fact. For example, Newton's view did not explain electricity and magnets very well. Let's take a look now at electromagnetism. We shall see how it differs from the mechanical view.

The story of electromagnetism begins with a simple experiment. In 1820, a scientist named

Hans C. Oersted set up the experiment. He ran an electric current from a battery through a wire. Then he pulled a compass out of his pocket. He set it near the wire. The needle of the compass jumped a bit. It turned away from pointing north. The needle was pointing in the same direction that the electric current was flowing. Remember how Albert's compass needle never moved, no matter how he turned it? Well, since the needle in his experiment moved toward the wire, Oersted learned that electricity could create magnetism. But his results led to a new question: Could magnetism create electricity?

Michael Faraday tried to answer this question. In 1831, he built a machine that could quickly rotate magnets. As the magnets moved, an electric current flowed through a wire. Yes, magnetism could create electricity. The work of Oersted and Faraday showed that magnetism and electricity are two aspects of one force. We call that force electromagnetism.

Electromagnetism was much different from any force that Newton had described. Remember that for Newton, objects were attracted to each other depending on their size and distance from each other. Also, Newton measured distance using a straight line. Into the 1860s, scientists learned more about electromagnetism. James Clerk Maxwell saw that the force of electromagnetism could not be measured using a straight line. Electric waves and magnetic waves flow at right angles to each other, not a straight line. The space around the two waves seems to vibrate. The space is part of the force. Maxwell called this space a field.

In Newton's view, empty space played no role. The space between objects did not influence the attraction. But in electromagnetism it did. So electromagnetism seemed to describe a force much different from the mechanical one.

Einstein turned over in his mind the ideas of Newton and Maxwell. He fretted and wondered. Could the two different forces be explained in a unified way? He looked at that problem from various angles. He thought about space, time, and distance. He also thought about light.

A view of Bern, Switzerland. In Bern, Albert Einstein developed his Special Theory of Relativity and his Photon Theory of Light.

Einstein knew that Maxwell had also thought about the nature of light. Maxwell had realized that light was similar to electromagnetism. He correctly assumed that light waves are types of electromagnetic waves.

But if light travels in waves, what does it travel through? Waves on a pond travel through water. Waves of sound travel through air. But light from a distant star travels through empty space. Scientists simply could not imagine a wave traveling through emptiness.

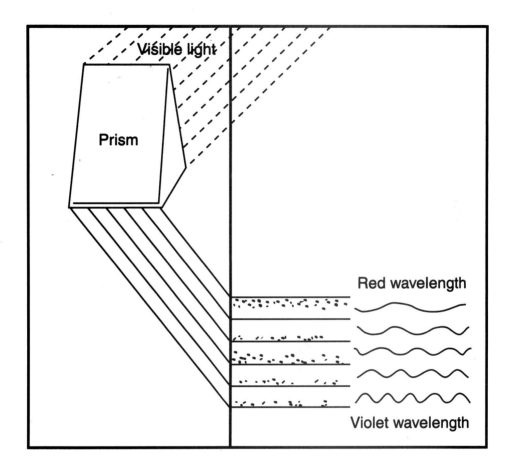

Light travels in waves of different lengths and colors. Visible light can be separated by a prism into different wavelengths. Red is the longest wavelength and violet is the shortest. The colors from longest to shortest are: red, orange, yellow, green, blue, indigo and violet.

4

Photons of Light Dancing in His Head

WAVES OR PARTICLES? PARTICLES OR waves? That is a key question that scientists asked about light in 1905. Scientists are still asking that question today. Light can behave like waves and particles. James Clerk Maxwell had supposed that light travels in waves. Newton assumed that light traveled as tiny particles. As he worked at the patent office, Einstein asked himself the question again and again. Particles or waves? Waves or particles?

How had Maxwell shown that light behaves like a wave? Well, light can bend; so can waves. Try shining a thin beam of light in the dark

James Clerk Maxwell (1831–1879) believed that light traveled in waves. His theories, however, were unable to describe all aspects of light.

through a pinhole. The reflection on the wall appears as rings of dark and light. This pattern is typical of a wave.

However, Maxwell's wave theory could not explain other behaviors of light. For example, scientists tried shining beams of light on metals. A mild electric current flowed. That meant that the light forced the metal atoms to lose electrons. This event is called the photoelectric effect. Atoms are the basic building blocks of elements. Atoms are made up of electrons, neutrons, and protons. The way that the light loosened the electrons did not seem wavelike.

Einstein thought about this problem by making an analogy. An analogy is a comparison. Einstein used a wooden sea wall, sea waves, and bullets to make his analogy.[1]

Imagine that the sea wall is like the sheet of metal. The waves of the sea are like waves of light. And the bullets are like particles of light. First imagine the waves rolling up against the sea wall. With time, the sea wall will wear down. Can you picture what will happen to the sea wall? Parts of it will wash away. Its wood will splinter. The wall will thin out in places, and it will warp.

But now imagine another scene. A spray of bullets hits a sea wall. Can you picture how different the sea wall will look this time? Holes will be all over. In both cases, the sea wall has lost mass. But in each case, the look will be much different.

In 1900, Max Planck explained the way metal gives off energy when it is heated. He noticed that the heat radiated is similar to bullets flying from a wall. The heated metal gave off little bundles of energy. When the heat got stronger, the energy still flew off in little bundles.

Planck called the little bundles of energy quanta. Einstein thought about Planck's work a lot. Maybe Planck's ideas about heat could be true for light. After all, both heat and light had color. The color of heat changes from red to orange to yellow to white. Its color depends on its temperature.

Einstein tried to better understand what Planck meant by little bundles of energy. Planck called this energy noncontinuous. Einstein thought of another analogy to help him understand what Planck meant by "noncontinuous." This time he used a city map to make his comparison.[2]

Spread a city map on the table before you. With a red marker, mark the route from your house to school. Now imagine that you travel to school on a city bus. With a green marker, mark all the bus stops. You will have several green dots, right? The bus stops in several specific places. Each dot is separate. Now pretend that you travel to school in a car. With a purple marker, mark all the places the car could stop. The car might stop anywhere, correct? Unlike a bus driver, the car's driver does not have to make specific stops. The driver just stops wherever he or she pleases. Your purple marker will follow the entire route. You will draw a line, not a series of dots. The line is continuous; the dots are noncontinuous.

Here is another example. Imagine milk in a huge milk machine. You press the button and the milk fills a huge five-gallon container. The milk fits evenly. Right to the brim. Now imagine milk in small half-pint cartons. You begin to pile the small cartons into the huge container. The fit might not be perfect. After all, you cannot tear the carton in half to make it fit in the container evenly. If you do, you'll have a big mess on your hands! The cartons are separate units. They are noncontinuous.

Thinking about continuous and non-continuous events helped Einstein clarify his ideas about light. In 1905, he wrote a paper about the photoelectric effect. He applied Planck's ideas to light. Light has a dual nature according to Einstein. At the very same time, it is like both particles and waves. Light is a shower of particles with some traits of a wave. He called the tiny particles photons. Einstein made a chart to show the difference between waves and photons.[3]

Wave Theory: Each color of light has a definite wavelength. The wavelength of red is twice that of violet.

Photon Theory: Each color of light has a

definite bundle of energy. The bundle of energy for red is half that of violet.

In other words, Einstein joined ideas of wave theory and particle theory. Particles or waves? Waves or particles? Einstein's answer was photons.

You should understand that Einstein worked out his ideas in his head. He had no laboratory in which he could experiment. Science involves many activities, but mainly thought, observation, and experimentation. Einstein greatly depended on pure thought. He called his work thought experiments. He made analogies and created images to explain things. Other scientists carried out experiments. Their experiments often proved Einstein right.

Scientists applauded the ideas of both Planck and Einstein. Both men had dared to take a leap in the dark. Both had imagined energy in a new way. In 1918, Planck won a Nobel Prize for his quanta theory. In 1921, Einstein won a Nobel Prize for his photon theory. But as Einstein accepted the prize, he did not feel perfectly

Albert Einstein won a Nobel Prize in 1921 for his photon theory of light.

happy. He did not feel that his work on photons was his best work. After all, he had used the ideas of Planck.

During his Nobel speech, Einstein did not speak of photons. He spoke of relativity. He wanted the audience to know of his greatest theory. Relativity has to do with the speed of light. Einstein thought it would change the way scientists thought about time, about distance, and about speed. It would also change their ideas about mass and about energy. And they would be able to think about acceleration and about gravity in a new way. However, for a long time, no one paid attention to the patent clerk's novel ideas about relativity.

Trains Zipping By

ONE DAY IN 1904, ALBERT EINSTEIN boarded a street car in Bern, Switzerland. He had a lot on his mind—light and time, Maxwell and Newton, patents, new inventions, paperwork, photons, math formulas, and many unanswered questions. He looked up out the train window at a clock. He allowed his imagination to roam. He amused himself with a new thought experiment. Suppose the street car suddenly zipped away from the clock at the speed of light. Wouldn't the hands on the clock look as if they had stopped? After all he would be moving from them on the crest of a

City Hall, Bern, Switzerland. Albert Einstein imagined that if he traveled at the speed of light away from a clock, the hands on the clock might stand still.

light wave. But his own watch would be safe in his pocket. It probably would tick in its regular way.[1]

Of course, Einstein had no real proof that his daydream wasn't just silly. Still, it made him wonder. Shouldn't he at least consider the possibility? Maybe time was not absolute. It was worth thinking about. His radical ideas about time might help solve some puzzles. So many things just did not make sense. Take all the talk about ether, for instance.

Ever since Maxwell's experiments, scientists had been talking a lot about ether. What was it? Remember that scientists did not understand how light flowed through empty space. So they guessed that maybe space was not empty. Maybe a gas really filled space. They called this gas ether. Maybe it allowed the light to travel. But this idea created a problem. No one could feel, measure, or weigh ether. No one could taste, smell, of hear it either. So did it really exist?

Maxwell's studies caused another uproar as well. He had used the speed of light in his formulas. Light travels at about 186,000 miles per second. But how could its speed be constant? Wouldn't it change with the frame of reference? You are probably scratching your head. What in the world is frame of reference? What does that mean?

Imagine that you are swimming upstream in a river. You measure the speed of the current. Now imagine that you are standing on the river shore. Again, you measure the speed of the current. Are your measurements the same? No, of course not. When you are swimming in the opposite direction, the current passes by you more swiftly.

In the first case, your frame of reference is your moving body. In the second case, it is the shore. What was Einstein's frame of reference as he looked at the clock? The zooming street car, of course. So frame of reference has to do with where you are. It also has to do with how fast you move as you see events.

For a long time, scientists had talked about frame of reference. Galileo had experimented with it. He came up with an interesting observation. He said that when you move smoothly, you can't tell that you are moving at all.

Have you noticed that? You are sitting on a parked train. You are waiting for it to start. You look out the window. You see another train parked next to yours. Suddenly that train starts to move. Or maybe it is your train. You cannot be sure at first.

Galileo showed us that most events seem the same for us if we move or are still. For example, suppose you drop a book from your lap as you sit in a train. It falls as if you were sitting in a chair at home. Also time will seem the same in both places. Distance will seem the same. But speed for Galileo worked a bit differently.

Roll a ball down the middle aisle of your train. The train is traveling at sixty miles per hour. The ball rolls slowly—five miles per hour. You measure the speed of the ball. Your answer? It's five miles per hour, of course.

But let's suppose you have a friend standing on a platform. Her name is Susan and she is waiting for another train. As you whisk by her,

Susan sees your ball rolling. So she adds the speed of the train to the speed of the ball. She adds sixty miles per hour plus five miles per hour. Her answer is sixty-five miles per hour. Her answer is much different from yours. So frame of reference makes a difference with speed.

Now let's return to Maxwell and the confusion he caused. Remember, Maxwell had measured the electromagnetic force. His formula included the speed of light. He had noticed that it took time for electricity to flow. Newton had not used time with his formulas. He thought forces attracted at once. But Maxwell noticed a slight delay in reactions. This delay seemed to match the speed of light.

But which speed of light did he mean? From what frame of reference? Would his answers be different if he were standing on the platform as Susan was? Would they be different if he were on the express train with you? It just did not make sense if his answers changed. After all, math is the same everywhere. Two plus two equals four—no matter if you are traveling on a ship, airplane, train, or stubborn mule! Two plus two equals four—that's all there is to it!

Maxwell's calculations seemed to work. They described the force of electromagnetism well. But what about the speed of light? Could it always be the same, no matter what? Some scientists tried to brush away the problem. "Maybe it's the ether," they said. Every time they couldn't understand something, that was their reply.

Remember the fairy tale by Hans Christian Andersen called "The Emperor's New Clothes"? All the town's people knew that an emperor was supposed to wear fancy clothes. They also knew that all emperors liked to be praised. These ideas clouded everybody's judgment. They doubted their own eyes. They thought they should see new clothes on the emperor, so they said they did. It took a bold and honest lad to set the people straight. "The emperor has no clothes," that daring lad yelled. Suddenly, everybody knew that he was right. They laughed at their own foolishness and at the naked emperor!

Albert Einstein was like that daring lad. It was

as if he suddenly yelled, "There is no ether!" And everyone knew he might be right. And maybe, just maybe, light goes as fast as anything can go. Frame of reference doesn't change its speed! Einstein dared to think that thought. It turned the whole world upside down.

Think about this: speed and time and distance are related. Divide the distance an object has moved, by the amount of time it took to travel that distance. This will give you the speed the object was traveling at. Speed (S) equals distance (D) divided by time (T) ($S = D/T$). But what if speed is constant? If the speed of light is constant, then what? Then we will have to ask some new questions about time and distance. Is time the same for everybody? Is distance?

Don't worry, don't pull your hair, and don't bite your fingernails! Einstein's ideas don't affect our ordinary ideas of time and distance. After all, we don't scuttle around at the speed of light. It is hard for us to imagine life in that super-fast lane. We think that five minutes is five minutes. Maybe we are shooting by in a bullet train. Maybe we are standing on our heads on a mountaintop. Or maybe we are doing wheelies at the bottom of the ocean. In any case five minutes is five minutes.

It's not exactly true that five minutes is five minutes. But it might as well be true. For our lives are very very slow compared to the speed of light—even if we break marathon records or race the Indianapolis 500! We are simply too slow to notice changes in measuring time.

Einstein helped us to understand a world in which time is not absolute. He drew a picture of a train. Remember that in Einstein's day, everybody rode trains to get places. Einstein often used them to picture ideas. New ideas are easier to understand if we first think of something we know. So Einstein thought about trains. They carried him quickly to very new territory.[2]

Look at the diagram of the train on page 66. You can see that we have two frames of reference or points of view. We have the frame of reference of the person on the train, whose name is Sam. And we have the frame of reference of Susan, waiting on the platform.

THE TIME MUSEUM

Einstein used a flashlight and mirror for a clock to illustrate his Special Theory of Relativity. At the Time Museum in Rockford, Illinois, you can see that many devices are used as clocks.

Einstein asks us to think of a clock as the flashlight and mirror. You can see them in the diagram. Such a clock might seem odd. Can a flashlight and mirror be a clock? It seems impossible at first. But it is not. After all almost anything can be a clock—an hour glass, a sundial, a water device, an atom. People have used many objects as clocks. What makes a clock a clock? A clock measures a unit of time. So what does the light clock measure? It measures the unit of time of a round trip beam of light. The light leaves the flashlight, which is on the floor. The beam travels to the mirror, which is on the ceiling. The light is then reflected from the mirror. It goes back down to the floor. The round trip is our unit of time.

In the diagram you can see the round trip of light for two people—Sam and Susan. Sam is on the train traveling with the clock. So the light makes the round trip in straight lines. Susan is not on the train. First the train is in front of her. So she sees the light go up in a straight line. But then the train darts by. Susan then sees the return trip of light at an angle. The round trip of light for Susan is longer than for Sam. So Susan thinks Sam's clock has slowed down. This example paints a picture to help us understand. It is only an imaginary example. A train goes way too slow to make a difference when measuring time.

But consider this. Time is different in different

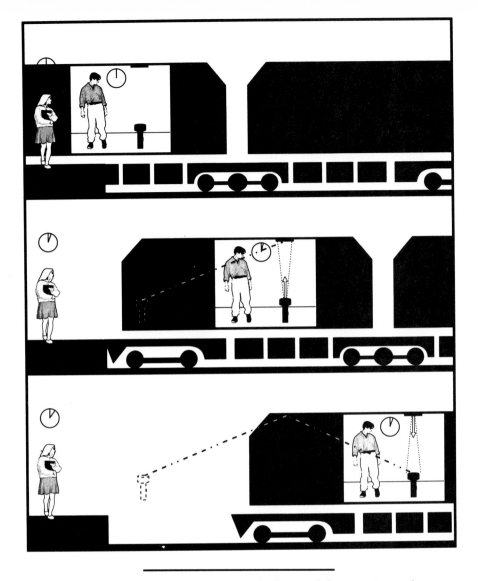

Susan stands on the train station platform, while Sam is on the train. The time for both is noon. A flashlight on the floor of the train is aimed at a mirror on the ceiling. As Sam's train takes off at near the speed of light, the beam from the flashlight makes the trip to the mirror in its normal time. There is no apparent difference. From Susan's point of view though, the distance the light must travel (dashed line) increases since the train is moving at nearly the same speed as the beam of light. The same is true when the beam is reflected back by the mirror, and the time difference between what Susan sees and what Sam sees becomes even greater.

frames of reference. If so, we must realize something new. The word "now" depends on where we are. In other words, there is no "now"—only "here and now." Remember this refrain: "No now. Only here and now." Repeat it five times, or at least three!

What would happen if we could see someone traveling near the speed of light? We would notice many strange things. Their time would seem different from ours and so would their distance. Einstein's idea about speed and time and distance is called the special theory of relativity.

Einstein's theory made sense logically. But Einstein knew it was not complete. So far he had looked only at two frames of reference. He had looked at the platform. He had looked at the smoothly moving train. He had imagined Susan standing still. But nobody ever really stands still. Did you know that? You might think that you can stand still. But you rotate with the earth on its axis at about 1,000 miles per hour. And you revolve with the earth around the sun at about 67,000

Albert Einstein used the image of a train to explain the relativity of time. In the painting above, the artist also used a train and a clock to give us a message about time.

miles per hour. And that is not all! You also circle with the solar system around the galaxy. This happens at an amazing speed—about 178 miles per second. And you even go with the galaxy as it expands with the universe. Nobody ever truly stands still!

Freely Falling in Space

ONE DAY IN 1914, A GERMAN WORKER WAS fixing a roof on a shed. He stumbled and fell from the roof. Onlookers ran up to him to see if he was okay. One of those who ran to help was a professor at the University of Berlin. Fortunately the worker did not get hurt. His fall had left him puzzled though. As he floated down he felt no force pulling him. He felt as though he were freely falling in space. He told those around him about his experience.[1]

"That was the happiest moment of my life," Einstein later remarked. Yes, the professor who

Berlin in the 1920s was one of the largest cities in Europe. It was a great center of culture and learning.

helped the worker had been Albert Einstein. He had been invited to Germany to work on physics.

Why was the worker's statement the happiest moment in Einstein's life? The remark helped Einstein think about gravity in a new way. Remember that he longed to apply his ideas about relativity to all movement. He needed to rethink gravity. Newton had said gravity attracted. But maybe it did not after all.

One day Einstein had a daydream that helped him form a new theory of gravity.[2] He imagined an elevator with no windows falling freely in space. A man floated in the elevator. He was weightless. Think of the man in the elevator dropping a ball. The ball would be weightless too. It would float next to him. It would not fall to the floor.

Einstein then imagined a crane driving up to the elevator. The crane hooked onto the top of the falling elevator. It pulled it up. The man was now moving upward. Suddenly, the man was standing on the floor. When he dropped the ball, it fell to the floor. He and the ball no longer weighed nothing. The man probably would think that gravity now ruled. The man inside had no idea what was going on. The elevator had no windows. So he could not see the crane.

Einstein's thought experiment shows something amazing. The upward force created by the crane and the force of gravity act the same way. Gravity is like an elevator floor coming up. It reaches all objects at the same time. The upward force of the crane is like acceleration. Acceleration is gathering or losing speed. The acceleration of the elevator created a force like gravity. Thus, Einstein showed that they are the same.

Thoughts about gravity led to thoughts about space. Einstein remembered Maxwell's experiments with electromagnetism. Space around electromagnetic waves vibrates. Maxwell called this vibrating space a field. Could space be a field rather than empty? Could space be related to gravity? Einstein thought so.

Picture a mountain with a castle on top. Everyone in the kingdom wants to travel to the castle to get the king's blessing. They walk all night to arrive by dawn. All citizens carry lanterns and walk along paths. All paths lead to the top of the mountain.[3]

Now imagine the view from an airplane. From an airplane all you can see are dots of light moving toward the mountaintop. You do not see the paths. So the mountaintop seems to just attract everyone to it. Do you see the comparison? The airplane view is like the mechanical view. The mountaintop is like gravity—it attracts all objects to it.

But with dawn we see what is really going on. In the daylight, we see that the mountaintop is not drawing citizens to it. Rather, the people walk along paths. In Einstein's view, gravity is like the paths. But now we must ask a question. What make paths in space? Planets and stars and other heavenly bodies do.

Now think of space as a sheet of plastic spread tight. Place weights on top of the plastic. The weights are like planets and stars. Can you picture what happens to the plastic? It becomes warped, right? It curves around the weights. If you were to roll a marble on the plastic, what would happen? It would roll toward the weights. It would follow the curves in the plastic. These curves are like paths; they are the paths of gravity.

Einstein thought about these ideas for years. He made comparisons using elevators and plastic sheets. But he also used the math formulas of Maxwell. And he used the math from his own special theory of relativity. He predicted that light would bend as it came near a body in space. He also predicted that time would slow down near gravity or with acceleration.

Einstein called his new ideas the general theory of relativity. He called it "general" because it applied to the whole universe. It applied to all frames of reference. But was Einstein right?

Scientists wanted to prove Einstein either right or wrong. But scientists could not experiment very well in space in the early 1900s. However they did find out one thing. Einstein's formulas correctly charted the orbit of Mercury. Mercury is the planet closest to the Sun. So its path is greatly affected by

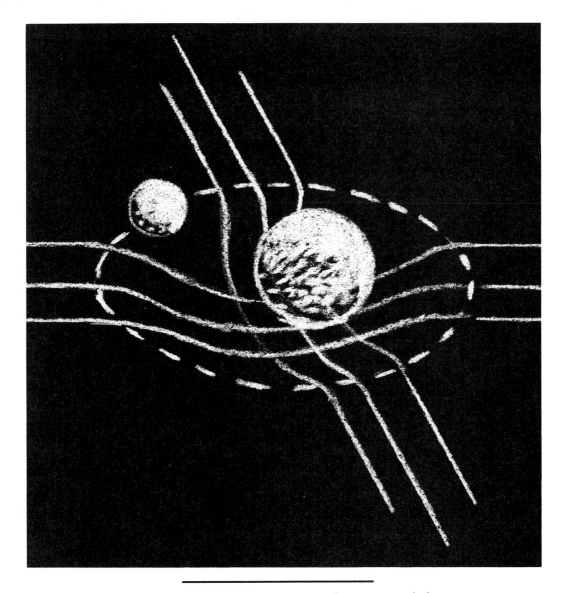

A simple representation of the curvature of space around the sun. The heavy ball at the center of the sheet represents the sun; the small ball represents the earth.

Albert Einstein worked in Berlin from 1914 to 1933. He developed his General Theory of Relativity there in 1915.

the Sun's warping of space. Newton's formulas had worked for all the planets except Mercury.

Actually, Newton's and Einstein's formulas turn out the same for most events. We still use Newton's ideas to describe ordinary events on earth. But when describing unusual events, Newton's view falls apart. Einstein's view holds up.

After a while scientists found out that Einstein's predictions about the bending of light could be observed. Look at the diagram on page 79. It shows a star behind the sun. Stars behind the sun can be seen during an eclipse. Then, the glare of the sun does not block them out. Notice that the star appears to be to the left of its actual position. How do scientists know the actual position? Because the earth revolves around the sun. So the stars all around the sun can be charted. The diagram shows a visual twist. It is due to star light bending toward the sun.

Also, experiments with time show Einstein right. Scientists can now measure time using precise atomic clocks. Time is slower at sea level than on a mountaintop. In other words, gravity slows time down. Don't worry, the difference is only a few nanoseconds. (A nanosecond is a billionth of a second.)

Since acceleration is the same as gravity, it slows down time too. Some scientists have imagined that super-fast space travel might slow down time for passengers. Consider the "twin

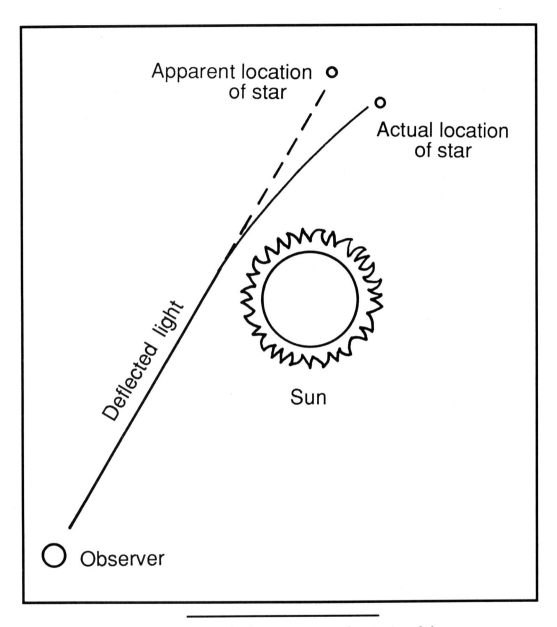

Star light bends towards the sun. Due to the gravity of the sun, the light of stars behind the sun bends, so they appear to the left of their actual position.

paradox." You go on a long space trip, traveling almost as fast as light. Your twin stays at home on earth. When you return, you will be younger than your twin! How much younger? Maybe a few weeks. Maybe a few years. That depends on how much speed you gathered on your journey. It also depends on how long you were gone. Of course, no one can travel that fast now. But the twin paradox is fun to think about.

So are black holes. Einstein's theory predicted strong gravity. If gravity gets very strong, light cannot escape. Time stops completely. Black holes are places of very strong gravity. Think again about the plastic sheet. Put an extremely heavy weight on the sheet. What will happen? The plastic will sink with the weight. And then the two edges of plastic will be drawn together. It is as though space closes in on itself. Try this experiment to see for yourself. Think of the heavy weight as a black hole.

Einstein's general theory of relatively makes us wonder. True we do not usually use it. We do not travel at the speed of light. We do not visit

This is how a black hole might look if you encountered one in space. The large number of stars near it is an optical illusion caused by the extreme curvature of space around it.

black holes. Most of us don't have to chart the orbit of Mercury. And we probably have never come home younger than our twin!

We walk to work or school. We listen to the news. We play ball, jog, or bicycle. We dance, sing, and shout. We eat breakfast every morning and supper every night. But sometimes we are alone and quiet. We look at the stars. Then our lives seem a small part of a great and wondrous universe.

The Conscience of a Scientist

$E = MC^2$. YOU PROBABLY HAVE HEARD OF this equation. Maybe you do not know what it means. But still you have heard and maybe seen it. Maybe you have seen it on a T-shirt. Maybe you have seen it scribbled on a blackboard. Maybe you have heard it in a joke. One cartoon shows Albert Einstein at a blackboard. He writes $E = ma^2$. No, no, that's wrong. He crosses it out. Then he writes $E = mb^2$. No, no, that's wrong too. He crosses it out. Finally, he writes $E = mc^2$. Eureka! Yes, that's it![1]

This joke, of course, is silly. E, in the equation stands for energy, m, stands for mass, and c, stands for the speed of light. All of these letters are a matter of choice. The letters themselves are not important. What is important is the idea. Einstein did not come to the idea by scribbling different letters on a blackboard. But how did he come to the idea? And what does it mean?

We will answer those questions in a moment. But first, we have some catching up to do. We last left Einstein in 1914 in Germany. He was thinking about gravity. And he was rescuing workers falling from sheds. Actually, the story about the worker and the shed may not be quite true. Stories about Einstein and his discoveries abound. Many of the stories make important points. But probably they are only partly true. Be that as it may. We do know that in 1914 Einstein returned to Germany. Kaiser Wilhelm II had invited him to work at the University of Berlin. He also invited him to become a member of Kaiser Wilhelm Institute. Max Planck urged Einstein to accept these offers. Planck worked in Germany along with many other important physicists. He knew that Einstein's work would flourish there. Berlin was *the* center of scientific thought in the early 1900s. Einstein hesitated because of his hatred of the German military. When the new kaiser took power he dismissed Otto von Bismarck. But still, the military spirit thrived. Einstein finally accepted the offer though. He enjoyed much freedom in his new post. His family life, however, fell apart.

Mileva hated Germany. Their sons hated school almost as much as Albert had as a child. Finally Mileva left. She took the boys on a vacation back to Switzerland. Then World War I broke out. Mileva decided it best to stay with the boys in the peaceful land of the Swiss. The separation seemed the last straw. The troubled marriage broke up. In 1919, Mileva and Albert divorced.

In spite of these problems, Albert Einstein's work was going well. He tried to ignore the political turmoil around him. He avoided German military work by saying that he was a Swiss citizen. Therefore, he said he must stay neutral. In his free time, Einstein found friendship at the home of his Uncle Rudolf. His cousin Elsa lived there with her two daughters. Like Albert, she too was divorced. The two cousins grew close and in time married. Elsa loved caring for Albertle, as she called him. She enjoyed cooking for him. Meanwhile, Einstein's growing fame irritated him. He hated all the media attention. Elsa, however, relished it. She took care of social obligations. So the marriage worked. Albert Einstein appreciated a stable home life enabling him to fully concentrate on physics.

Soon, however, trouble brewed. After World War I, Germany became more and more anti-Semitic. Soon, Albert Einstein found himself the target of verbal abuse. Up until this time, Albert Einstein did not think that much about being Jewish. Suddenly, he began to feel the prejudice directed against all Jews. He became more sympathetic to the political ideas of Zionism. Zionists wanted to find a place where Jews could live together in peace. They wanted a homeland.

By 1933, the Nazis controlled political life in Germany. It was only a matter of time before war

Albert Einstein left Germany in 1933 because of Nazi leader Adolf Hitler's growing power.

would rage. Einstein fled Germany, accepting a job at the Institute for Advanced Study in Princeton, New Jersey. He appreciated the peacefulness of his new home. But he could not forget the terrors of the Nazis. He watched in horror as Nazis persecuted Jews. Einstein always had prided himself on being a pacifist. (A pacifist is totally against all wars.) But now, Einstein could no longer be a pacifist. He felt that the horror of Nazism had to be stopped.

Einstein was alarmed when the Nazis invaded Czechoslovakia. He knew that Czechoslovakia mined great quantities of uranium. The Nazis forbade any export of uranium. Einstein realized that this was an ominous sign. Before long he wrote a letter to President Roosevelt. He urged the President to develop the atomic bomb. To understand why, we must now return to where we began. We must return to the famous formula.

$E = mc^2$ did not lead directly to the building of the atomic bomb. But the formula did lead scientists to think about splitting the atom. The formula suggested that splitting an atom would release a great deal of energy. When mass becomes energy, it does so with great zest. C equals the speed of light (186,000 miles per second). You know that the speed of light is a huge number. The square of the speed of light is a colossal number. (When we square something, we multiply it by itself.) The formula says that energy from mass must be multiplied by the speed of light squared.

We know that Einstein did not form this equation by scribbling letters on a blackboard. He did not cross out a and b. When he came to c, he did not yell, Eureka! But how did Einstein form the equation? He used logic and a thought experiment.

$E = mc^2$ comes from the special theory of relativity. Remember what the special theory of relativity says about the speed of light? It assumes that nothing moves as fast as the speed of light. Einstein imagined an object moving faster and faster. Then he asked a question. What prevents it from reaching the speed of light? Einstein guessed that the object would become more massive. It would be more difficult to move. The energy to move it would become greater and greater. Mass and energy are simply two aspects of the same thing. This was the line of reasoning that Einstein used. Then he worked out the idea mathematically. The math to show the formula is complicated. But the idea is logical.

In order to understand the idea better, we should talk about mass. What is it? We usually think mass is weight, but that is not exactly true. Weight depends on gravity while mass does not. Think of mass as the amount of force necessary to move something. Think of a marble and a bowling ball. If you push them both with the same force, which will move farther? The marble, of course. Why? Because it has less mass. Einstein imagined the marble being pushed with greater and greater force. It rolls along at great speed. It gathers more and more speed, but eventually it will gather no more. Why? Because it will gain mass. As it approaches the speed of light, its mass will be enormous. A marble's mass can be greater than the mass of a bowling ball—much much greater. It all depends on how fast it is moving. Don't bother trying this, however. It does not matter how good you are at shooting marbles. You simply cannot shoot them near the speed of light!

Einstein's formula had enormous potential—and not just for marbles! Scientists started to think about energy in a new way. Mass and energy were the same thing. A tremendous amount of energy lay hidden everywhere—in every acorn, every blade of grass, and every atom. Why don't we notice the energy? Because it is not given off. Einstein compared the hidden energy to a rich man. This rich man does not spend or give away any of his money. He does not live in a fancy house and wear elegant clothes. So no one knows he is rich. In the same way, we cannot tell that all matter is rich with energy.[2] But Einstein showed that it was. So scientists wondered about it. Maybe they could harness atomic energy. They wanted to find practical uses for it.

Unfortunately, it soon seemed that the first use of atomic energy might be destructive. Einstein knew that the uranium atoms were unstable, which made them fairly easy to split, releasing a great amount of energy. In 1938, two German chemists split a uranium nucleus in two by bombarding it with part of an atom called a neutron. Nuclear fission was possible. (Fission means splitting.) Could fission produce a chain reaction? Could one fission cause another and another? If so, tremendous energy would explode. Einstein feared that the Nazis were on to nuclear fission. He especially thought so after Germany's invasion of Czechoslovakia and its hoarding of uranium. He quaked when he thought of Nazis harnessing atomic energy. Surely they would drop atomic bombs.

Because of his fear, Einstein wrote to President Franklin D. Roosevelt in 1939. He urged him to buy uranium from the Belgian Congo. He also suggested a project to see if a chain reaction were possible. This became known as the Manhattan Project. They discovered a chain reaction was possible, and the first atomic bomb was born. Because of his letter to Roosevelt, Einstein came

Franklin D. Roosevelt dictates a letter to his secretary, Marguerite Le Hand. After Roosevelt received Einstein's letter, he ordered a project to develop the atomic bomb.

to be called the father of the atomic bomb. But Einstein resented this. It is true that his formula predicted great energy. And it is true that he wrote Roosevelt. But Einstein had nothing to do with the actual development of the bomb. He did not work on the Manhattan Project since he was not a nuclear physicist and did not have the know-how to work on the bomb.

In 1945 the United States dropped two atomic bombs on Japan.

In time Einstein regretted his letter to Roosevelt. He found that Germany had not made much progress with the bomb. So he wrote another letter to Roosevelt, begging him not to drop the bomb on Japan. But Roosevelt died before he could read this letter. In August 1945 President Truman decided to bomb Hiroshima and Nagasaki. He wanted to quickly end the war with Japan. Truman's decision greatly disappointed Einstein. He felt horrible. He compared himself to Alfred Nobel.[3] Nobel had invented dynamite. Then he dedicated himself to peace and he founded the Nobel Peace Prize. Einstein too was determined to spend much of the rest of his life working for peace.

In the Temple of Science

"I AM DEEPLY MOVED BY THE OFFER OF Israel. And at once saddened and ashamed that I cannot accept it."[1] Einstein wrote these words in 1952. Chaim Weizman, the first president of Israel, had just died. Now the people of Israel wanted Einstein to take his place.

Should he accept? Einstein had not forgotten the terrors of the war. After World War II, he worked for peace. He became chairman of the Emergency Committee of Atomic Scientists. He tried to control the spread of the atomic bomb. He also worked tirelessly for the new Jewish homeland. His speeches brought in needed funds for Israel. Now this offer seemed a reward for all his hard work.

Einstein realized though that he was not a politician. He decided to refuse. He explained that he was used to working with ideas and numbers, but he was not used to dealing with people. True, Einstein tried to improve the world for people. After the war he spoke out often, desiring a more humane world. But his first love was pure science. Einstein wanted to achieve another scientific goal before he died.

He dreamed of finding a unifying force in nature. Could one force describe all interactions of physics? Einstein thought so. But so far he had not found it. Remember that August Tuschmid had first inspired Einstein. Tuschmid had talked about the central problem of physics. He spoke of the two views known at that time—the mechanical view and the view of electromagnetism. Tuschmid had pointed out a need to unify these two views. Had Einstein been successful in doing so? Only partially.

Einstein's work had showed that the

mechanical view did not apply for all the universe. He introduced new ideas about gravity, space, and time. Space and time were not absolute. Gravity and acceleration were the same thing. In his theory of gravity, Einstein used the idea of the field. The field idea came from electromagnetism. But the two kinds of fields seemed different in many ways. But Einstein wanted to show that electromagnetism and gravity were really two aspects of one force. That was his dream. He worked for over thirty years on this problem. But it escaped him.

Meanwhile, new discoveries in quantum physics excited many scientists. Max Born, Niels Bohr, and others tried to figure out the nature of particles. Particles make up atoms and atoms make up all matter. Matter includes chairs and dogs, you and me, and all living and nonliving things. These scientists turned to the very, very small to try and understand the world. Einstein had looked at the very, very large universe. Actually, Einstein had studied both the small and the large. Both he and Max Planck did the first work in quantum physics.

Quantum physicists built on the ideas of Planck and Einstein. They realized that the idea of quanta did not apply only to heat and light. Particles, like those in atoms, also sometimes acted like waves. Werner Heisenberg worked out the math of the new theories. Soon he realized something amazing. Chance played a role. The actions of any particular particle were uncertain. It might do this, it might do that. Heisenberg said that we could talk about probability. But we could not talk about certainty. At least not when we spoke of particles. It was probable that they might act in a particular way, but not certain.

Heisenberg's work upset Einstein. He did not disagree with the math, but with the meaning. Heisenberg suggested that nothing was sure in the world. The design of the world no longer seemed perfect. "God does not play dice!" Einstein exclaimed.[2] He simply could not agree that chance had a role. Not in the laws of the universe!

Max Planck (1858–1947) founded quantum physics.

Then another revelation came about. Quantum scientists soon discovered two new forces. Gravity and electromagnetism were now no longer the only forces in the universe. In the nucleus of an atom, a strong force held protons and neutrons together. This third force, the strong force, was unlike anything ever observed before. It was stronger than both gravity and electromagnetism. But it did not act over great distances. That is why we do not notice it in everyday life.

A fourth force is called the weak force. It is stronger than gravity, but it is weaker than the strong force. And it is weaker than electro-magnetism. It has been observed during rare nuclear reactions.

These new discoveries astonished scientists. The very small world inside an atom surprised and bewildered them. The grand unifying theory grew distant. Four forces—not just two—had to be brought together.

Born and Bohr respected Einstein. They often asked his advice. But they could not understand why he was so stubborn. His idea of unifying seemed old-fashioned to them. Einstein had spent years looking for the one unifying force. He never found it. Someone once asked Einstein if it had been worth it. Einstein said, "At least I know ninety-nine ways that do not work."[3]

Today, many quantum scientists have returned to Einstein's idea. They search for a unifying force. And they have found theories that unite the weak force, the strong force, and electro-magnetism. Gravity still escapes them though. But they do not give up. Einstein's dream inspires them.

Einstein spent his remaining days in Princeton. He retired from the Institute for Advanced Study in 1945. Still, he continued his work. His doctors warned him that his heart was weak. But he would not rest.

Einstein had also become a very lonely man. Many of the people in his life were gone. His wife Elsa had died in 1936 and his sister Maja died in 1951. His health worsened.

In 1955, he was rushed into emergency

Albert Einstein remained active working for peace and science until his death in 1955.

surgery after complaining of stomach pains. A few days later, on April 18, the world's most famous scientist died. His body was cremated, and his ashes were scattered in a secret place.

Albert Einstein had sometimes compared science to a temple. He took that image from the Jewish religion. He did not practice Judaism, but the images of this religion stayed with him. "I can read the thoughts of God from Nature," he said.[4] He worked for a Jewish homeland, but he regarded his awe of nature as his only religion. He believed that true scientists entered "the temple of science." They entered not for money nor for fame. They entered for love. He himself had worked as a humble civil servant. As such he made his most startling discoveries. He was not being paid to be a scientist then. So he had felt free to work for love.

Students sometimes asked Einstein if they should follow a career in science. He gave this advice to a college student in California in 1951:

Science is a wonderful thing if one does not have to earn one's living at it. One should earn one's living by work of which one is sure one is capable. Only when we do not have to be accountable to anybody can we find joy in scientific endeavor.[5]

Einstein often answered letters not only from students, but from farmers, workers, and teachers. In these letters Einstein stressed the traits important to scientists. He wrote of independence, love, and dedication. He also wrote of curiosity and humility.

In 1947 an Idaho farmer wrote to Albert Einstein. He had some exciting news. The farmer had named his son Albert. Might Einstein write a few words for baby Albert to live by? Einstein wrote:

Nothing truly valuable arises from ambition or from a mere sense of duty; it stems rather from love and devotion towards men and towards objective things.[6]

These words delighted the farmer. He rewarded Einstein with a snapshot of his baby Albert. Also, Einstein found a huge bag of Idaho potatoes on his doorstep!

In addition, Einstein loved to write long letters to scientists. And he wrote essays about many,

Albert Einstein loved to write letters to scientists and ordinary people. He also wrote essays and books.

including Newton, Madame Curie, and Planck. Albert Einstein deeply respected Max Planck. He chose one of his favorite images to write about him—the holy temple. "Many kinds of men devote themselves to science. And not all for the sake of science herself," wrote Einstein. "There are some who come into her temple because it offers opportunity to display their particular talents."[7]

Einstein thought those who showed off their talent were like athletes. He thought those who wanted to make a lot of money were like businessmen. He feared that most scientists were like athletes and businessmen. But a few came to the temple of science to worship, inspired by love. Max Planck was one of those special few. Planck worshipped in the temple of science.

Perhaps we can imagine Einstein in the temple too. He sits quietly with his friend Max Planck and other great scientists. Maybe he is still thinking of *the* one unifying force. Maybe he is asking his impossible questions.

Activities

Activity One: Leaning Tower

Legend tells us that Galileo dropped two objects from the Leaning Tower of Pisa. In order to try his experiment, you will need a ladder and a friend with a stopwatch. You will also need two objects to drop. Make sure that they are objects of different weights and will not break. How about a softball and a baseball? Climb the ladder and drop the objects together. Have your friend time their fall. Do they land at the same time?

Activity Two: Needle Jump

Hans C. Oersted's experiment with electricity and a compass was an early step in the discovery of electromagnetism. In order to do a similar experiment, you will need a plastic or wooden ruler, a couple of feet of plastic-coated wire, a

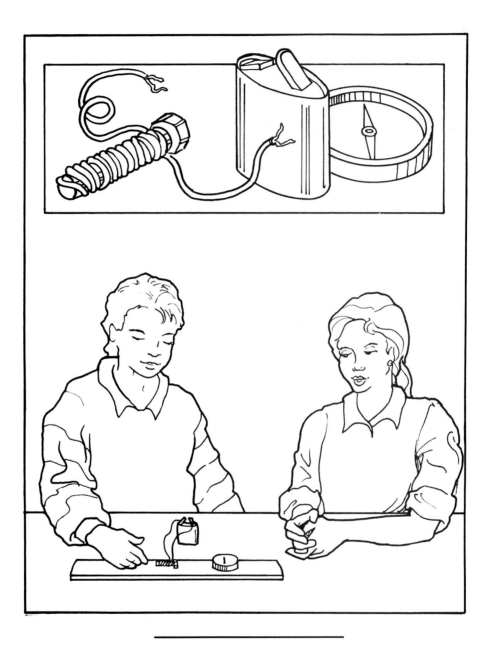

Make your own electromagnet.

small compass, a large iron bolt, and a 4.5-volt battery (see page 109).

Place the compass on one end of the ruler so that north is at the top. Then wind the wire many times around the bolt. Wind the wire in the same direction. Leave a few inches of wire free at each end. Place the bolt horizontally on the ruler. Place it near the compass. Connect the ends of the wire to the battery. Watch the compass needle. Does it jump toward the bolt? If it doesn't, move the bolt closer to the compass.

Activity Three: Seeing a Field with Your Own Eyes

In explaining electromagnetism, James Clerk Maxwell talked about fields. Later Einstein used the idea of field to describe gravity. But can we see a field? In a way we can. For this experiment you will need some magnets, iron filings, and a thin white piece of cardboard. If you do not have iron filings, you can make them. Simply file down a nail held in a vice. Put the sprinklings in a salt shaker.

First notice the location of the magnetic poles. Can you guess which is north or south? Make a note in your mind of their locations. Then lay the cardboard on the magnets. Next sprinkle the filings evenly on the cardboard. Tap the cardboard gently. Something amazing happens. The iron filings settle in a strange pattern. The pattern is the shape of the field. What exactly is going on? The filings are affected by the force of the poles of the magnets. The filings link opposite poles and avoid similar poles. The strength of these forces is stronger near the poles. Your filings have painted a magnetic picture. It shows that the field penetrates space in all directions.

Activity Four: Continuous and Separate

Particles, waves, and photons can be difficult to imagine. This activity may give you a clearer picture. You will need a large can of sand, some rocks, and water. You will also need a bucket, a dish towel, and a felt-tipped pen. Draw an even line around the bucket about half way up. Pour water in the bucket until it reaches the line. Can you pour the water so that it evenly reaches the line? The answer to that question is yes. You can think of water as continuous, like a wave.

Now empty the bucket and dry it with a towel. Pile rocks into the bucket until they reach the line. Can you pile rocks until they evenly reach the line? The answer will be no. Some of the rocks will jut over the line. You can think of rocks as separate, like particles.

Again empty the bucket. Now fill it with sand until the sand reaches the line. Can you fill the bucket until the sand evenly reaches the line? Yes, you can. Sand is continuous like the water. But it is separate like the rocks too. Why? Because if you look carefully, you can see separate grains. Sand is like photons; it is both continuous and separate!

Activity Five: Balloon Space

In Chapter Six, you read about Einstein's general theory of relativity. In that theory Einstein imagined space as curved. You can explore this idea by exploring the surface of a balloon. Blow a large balloon up about halfway. With the help of a friend and felt-tipped marker, mark the surface of the balloon with evenly spaced dots—maybe about six of them. These will represent galaxies in the universe. Circle one of the dots. This will represent our home galaxy the Milky Way. Measure the distance between the dots. Blow the balloon up more. Now measure the distance between the dots. Some scientists think our universe is closed space, similar to a balloon. The universe expands just like the balloon with more air. What happens then to the distance between galaxies?

Now, begin at the circled dot, the Milky Way. With your felt-tipped pen, draw a line as straight as possible. Continue drawing straight as possible, trying not to waver. What happens? You return to where you first started. If space is curved like a balloon, then a space traveler going in a straight line would return to where she first started.

How might we imagine black holes in balloon space? A black hole would be like a dimple on the surface of the balloon. Once the space traveler fell into the dimple she could not get out! Time would stop for her.

Chronology

1543—Nicolaus Copernicus published his theory that the earth revolves around the sun.

1600s—Galileo discovered important laws of motion.

1687—Sir Isaac Newton developed the laws of mechanics.

1820—Hans Christian Oersted discovered that electricity creates magnetism.

1831—Michael Faraday produced electricity with magnets.

1865—James Clerk Maxwell developed laws of electromagnetism.

1879—Albert Einstein was born in Ulm, Germany on March 14.

1900—Max Planck did his work in quantum physics.

1902—Albert Einstein began work at the Swiss Patent Office in Bern.

1903—Albert Einstein married Mileva Maric.

1905—Albert Einstein published papers on photons and the special theory of relativity.

1914—Einstein returned to Germany. Later that year World War I broke out.

1915—Einstein developed his general theory of relativity.

1919—Einstein divorced Mileva and married his cousin Elsa.

1922—The 1921 Nobel Prize in physics was awarded to Einstein.

1927—Werner Heisenberg developed his uncertainty theory about particles.

1933—Einstein left Germany for Princeton, New Jersey.

1939—Einstein wrote President Franklin D. Roosevelt, urging him to develop the atomic bomb.

1939—World War II begins.

1942—Enrico Fermi achieved the first controlled nuclear reaction.

1945—The United States dropped two atomic bombs on Japan (Hiroshima, August 6; Nagasaki, August 9). World War II ends.

1952—Einstein was asked to become the president of Israel, but declined the offer.

1955—Albert Einstein died at the age of seventy-six on April 18.

Notes by Chapter

Chapter One

1. The questions Einstein asked about the moon were chronicled by Abraham Pais in *Subtle Is the Lord: The Science and Life of Albert Einstein* (Oxford: Clarendon Press, 1982).

2. See *Albert Einstein, the Human Side: New Glimpses from his Archives.* Selected and edited by Helen Dukas and Banesh Hoffman. (Princeton, N.J.: Princeton University Press, 1979).

3. Ibid.

Chapter Two

1. Philip Frank in his book *Einstein: His Life and Times* (New York: Alfred H. Knopf, 1947) speaks of the military atmosphere in Germany and reports Einstein's response to it.

2. Albert Einstein tells about his reaction to the compass in his *Autobiographical Notes* (Peru, Ill.: Open Court Publishing Co., 1991).

3. Ibid.

4. Philip Frank. *Einstein: His Life and Times* (New York: Alfred H. Knopf, 1947).

5. Maja Einstein writes about her family and her

brother in a biography of 1924. It is included in *Collected Papers of Albert Einstein: The Early Years* (Princeton, N.J.: Princeton University Press, 1987).

6. The quote from Einstein's uncle is reported in many sources, including Philip Frank's book.

7. Einstein speaks of his love of geometry in *Autobiographical Notes.*

8. The quote from Einstein about school is reported in many sources, including Philip Frank's book.

9. *Einstein for Beginners* (New York: Pantheon Books, 1979) by Joseph Schwartz and Michael McGuinness has a good description of Germany's industrial growth in the 1880s.

Chapter Three

1. Besso's quote is reported in Philip Frank's *Einstein: His Life and Times* (New York: Alfred H. Knopf, 1947).

2. See "The Relative Importance of Mrs. Einstein" in *The Economist,* February 24, 1990.

3. Einstein's letters to Mileva are collected in *The Collected Papers of Albert Einstein, vol. 1 The Early Years* (Princeton, N.J.: Princeton University Press, 1987). The existence of Albert and Mileva's first child became known with the publication of this collection.

Chapter Four

1. Einstein and Leopold Infeld use the analogy

of the sea wall in *The Evolution of Physics* (New York: Simon and Schuster, 1938).

2. Ibid.

3. Ibid.

Chapter Five

1. The story of the streetcar is reported in Robert Hazen's and James Trefil's *Science Matters (New York: Doubleday, Anchor Books, 1991).*

2. The train and flashlight experiment is reported by Einstein in *Relativity: The Special and General Theory* (New York: Crown Books, 1961).

Chapter Six

1. The story about the worker is reported in many sources, including Nigel Calder's *Einstein's Universe* (New York: Penguin Books, 1979).

2. Einstein makes the analogy of the crane and elevator in *Relativity: The Special and General Theory* (New York: Crown Brooks, 1961).

3. The analogy of the mountaintop comes from Bertrand Russell, *The ABC of Relativity* (New York, Signet Books, 1958).

Chapter Seven

1. The cartoon described is by Sidney Harris, published in A. Zee's *Fearful Symmetry: The Search for Beauty in Modern Physics* (New York: Macmillan Publishing Company, 1986).

2. Einstein made the comparison of the rich man in *Out of My Later Years* (New York: Carol Publishing Group, 1956, 1984).

3. Albert Einstein talks about Albert Nobel in an essay of 1945 called, "The War Is Won But Peace Is Not." The essay can be found in the collection, Albert Einstein, *Essays in Humanism* (New York: Philosophical Library, 1950, 1983).

Chapter Eight

1. This quote is taken from a telegram Einstein sent Abba Eban cited in Ronald W. Clark's *Einstein: The Life and Times* (New York: Avon Books, 1953).

2. Einstein used the image of God playing dice in his letters to Max Born. *The Born-Einstein Letters* translated by Irene Born (New York: Walker & Company, 1971).

3. This quote is cited in *Einstein's Dream* by Barry Parker (New York: Plenum Press, 1986).

4. This quote is taken from William Hermanns' *Einstein and the Poet: In Search of the Cosmic Man* (Brooklin Village, Mass.: Branden Press, 1983).

5. This quote is taken from a letter in the Einstein archives and collected in *Albert Einstein, The Human Side: New Glimpses from His Archives*. Selected and edited by Helen Dukas and Banesh Hoffman. (Princeton University Press, Princeton, N.J., 1979).

6. Ibid.

7. Einstein's praise of Planck can be found in Max Planck's *Where Is Science Going?* (Woodbridge, Conn.: Ox Bow Press, 1981).

Glossary

acceleration—An increase in the speed of an object. Einstein believed that acceleration and gravity behaved in the same way.

anti-Semitism—Prejudice against Jewish people. In Nazi Germany, prejudice turned to hate and murder, leaving six million Jews dead.

black hole—A theoretical space object of such enormous mass that it absorbs all light, heat, and radio waves.

civil servant—A government worker.

electromagnetism—One of the four forces found in nature. This force binds oppositely charged particles. At the most basic level, it is responsible for holding atoms together.

electron—Electrons are one of the three main particles that are found in atoms. They are found orbiting the nucleus of the atom and are negatively charged.

field—The space around an object that has been altered by a force, such as gravity or magnetism.

force—The interaction between particles. There

are four known forces in nature: electromagnetism, gravity, strong force, and weak force.

General Theory of Relativity—Einstein's theory that describes gravity. According to this theory, gravity depends on the curvature of space. The curves in space are caused by the mass of objects such as stars and planets.

geometry—A part of mathematics that studies lines, angles, and points, and how they fit together.

grand unifying theory—A scientific theory that would show that gravity, electromagnetism, the strong force, and the weak force are really just different forms of one force.

gravity—The force that holds heavenly bodies in their orbit and causes objects to fall. Newton thought this force worked by attraction. But Einstein thought that the curvature of space caused gravity.

gymnasium—In Germany, a secondary school that prepares young people for college.

Institute for Advanced Study—A community of scholars and scientists in Princeton, New Jersey, founded in 1930. Here, researchers can work without restrictions from a university or a government.

law—In science, a phenomenon that seems always to be true.

mass—The amount of matter in an object is roughly

roughly equal to its mass. On the earth, we speak of mass and weight as the same thing. In space, objects are weightless, but they still have mass.

mechanics—The field of physics in which scientists study objects in motion.

mechanics, Newtonian—The laws of motion, including gravity, established by Isaac Newton.

Nazism—A German political movement that led to World War II and the murder of six million Jews in Europe.

neutrons—Neutrons are one of the three main particles that are found in atoms. They are found in the nucleus, and have no electrical charge.

probability—The study of the likelihood of an event. For example, what are the chances a coin tossed will land on "tails"?

protons—Protons are one of the three main particles that are found in atoms. They are found in the nucleus, and have a positive electrical charge.

Prussia—A warlike German nation that ruled over north-central Europe for hundreds of years. Prussia united with other German states, but was crushed in World War I. After World War II (when Germany showed the same warlike qualities of Prussia), the name Prussia was officially abolished.

quantum mechanics—The study of objects in motion using quantum theory. Quantum mechanics helps us understand parts of nature that are not explained by Newton's Laws.

quantum theory—The theory that energy is made up of small packets called quanta. Light is a form of energy made of quanta called photons.

Special Theory of Relativity—Einstein's theory that describes our perception of objects in motion. According to this theory, the mass and size of objects changes when in motion. These changes become noticeable as the speed of the object approaches the speed of light (186,000 miles per second).

strong force—The force that holds atomic nuclei together. It binds neutrons and protons to one another. It is one of the four forces Einstein tried to unify in a single force.

weak force—The force that occurs within atoms during radioactive decay. It is one of the four forces Einstein tried to unify in a single force.

Further Reading

Apfel, Necia H. *It's All Relative: Einstein's Theory of Relativity.* New York: Lothrop, Lee & Shepard Books, 1981.

Berger, Melvin. *Our Atomic World.* New York: Franklin Watts, 1989.

Ireland, Karin. *Albert Einstein.* Englewood Cliffs, N.J.: Silver Burdett, 1989.

Reef, Catherine. *Albert Einstein: Scientist of the 20th Century.* Minneapolis: Dillon Press, 1991.

Riedman, Sarah R. *Men and Women Behind the Atom.* New York: Abelard–Schuman, 1958.

Stwertka, Albert and Eve. *Physics from Newton to the Big Bang.* New York: Franklin Watts, 1986.

Veglahn, Nancy. *Coils, Magnets, and Rings: Michael Faraday's World.* New York: Coward, McCann & Geohegan, Inc., 1976.

Wolf, Fred Alan. *Taking the Quantum Leap.* New York: Harper & Row, 1989.

Internet Addresses

Albert Einstein: Person of the Century

<http://www.time.com/time/time100/poc/home.html>

A. Einstein: Image and Impact

<http://www.aip.org/history/einstein/>

Einstein Revealed

<http://www.pbs.org/wgbh/nova/einstein/>

Time Travel: Think Like Einstein

<http://www.pbs.org/wgbh/nova/time/think.html>

Index

A

Aarau, Switzerland, 30–31
acceleration, 73, 78
anti-Semitism, 25, 86
atomic energy, 88–95

B

Berlin, Germany, 84–85
Berlin, University of, 70, 84
Bern, Switzerland, 32–34, 55
Besso, Michaelangelo, 34–35
Bismarck, Otto von, 18, 19, 28
black holes, 80, 114
Bohr, Niels, 98, 101
Born, Max, 98, 101

C

Catholic religion, 25
chance, 99
clocks, 55–57, 64–65, 78
compass, 23–25, 108–110
continuous vs. noncontinuous phenomenon, 50–52, 111–112
Copernicus, Nicolaus, 38

E

$E = mc^2$, 83–84, 88–91
Einstein, Albert
    in Berlin, Germany, 84–88
    in Bern, Switzerland, 32–36
childhood family life, 21–23
children, 36–37, 85
as civil servant, 34–35
correspondence, 13, 35–36, 103–105
death of, 102, 104
education, 25–31
first marriage, 35–37, 85
general theory of relativity, 70–82
as a genius, 12–13, 16
and the grand unifying theory, 97–102
letters to Roosevelt, 88, 92, 93
Nobel Prize awarded to, 53–54
photon theory, 48–54
political work, 95, 96–97
in Princeton, New Jersey, 7–13
second marriage, 85–86
special theory of relativity, 55–69
Einstein, Elsa, 85, 86, 102
Einstein, Hermann, 21–23, 29–30
Einstein, Jacob, 26, 28
Einstein, Maja, 21, 24, 102
Einstein, Mileva, 10, 35–37, 85

Einstein, Pauline, 21, 23
electricity, 29–30, 108–109.
    See also electromag-
    netism
electromagnetism, 42–45,
    61, 97, 101, 108–110
Emergency Committee of
    Atomic Scientists, 96
energy. *See* $E = mc^2$
ether, 57, 61

F
Faraday, Michael, 42
Federal Polytechnic Academy
    (Switzerland), 10, 30, 34
fields, 43, 73, 110, 111
forces of nature, 101
frame of reference, 58–60,
    62, 63, 67–69
Franco-Prussian War, 19

G
Galileo, 39, 58–59, 108
Germany
    industrial growth of, 29–30
    military parades in, 17–
    19, 21
    military strength of, 19
    and Nazism, 86–88
grand unifying theory, 97–102
gravity
    Einstein's ideas, 72–82
    Newton's ideas, 39–41

H
Haller, Friedrich, 35
Heisenberg, Werner, 99

I
Israel, 96–97

J
Jewish customs, 25–26, 104

L
light
    and electromagnetism, 44
    particles or waves, 46–54
    speed of, 55, 57–58, 60–
    69. *See also* $E = mc^2$

M
magnets, 23, 25. *See also*
    electromagnetism
Manhattan Project, 92–93
Marr, Wilhelm, 25
mass. *See* $E = mc^2$
mathematics, 13, 26–28, 60–61
Maxwell, James Clerk, 110
    formulas of, 57–58, 60–61
    ideas of electromagnet-
    ism, 43, 44, 46
    ideas of light, 44, 46–48
mechanical view. *See* physics.
Mercury (planet), 14, 75
Munich, Germany, 21

N
Nazism, 86–88
Newton, Isaac, 13–14, 31
    ideas about light, 46
    law of gravity, 39–41
Nobel Prize, 53–54

O
Oersted, Hans C., 42, 108
Olympia Academy, 11

P
Pais, Abraham, 10, 11
photon theory, 45–54
physics. *See also* relativity
    central problem, 31, 37,
    97
    grand unifying theory,
    97–102
    history of, 37–45

mechanical view, 13–14, 31, 37, 39–41
quantum, 49–50, 51, 53, 98–102
Planck, Max, 49–50, 51, 53–54, 99, 100, 107
Princeton, New Jersey, 7–13
probability, 99
Prussia, 19–*20*

Q
quantum physics, 49–51, 53, 98–102

R
relativity
    general theory of, 70–82, 114
    special theory of, 55–69, 112–113
Roosevelt, Franklin D., 88, 92, 93

S
science
    advances in the 1800s, 14

compared to temple, 102, 104, 107
history of, 37–45
laws of, 39
speed, 62. *See also* light, speed of
Swabia, 21
Swiss Patent Office, 34–35

T
Talmey, Max, 26
time, 34, 62–69, 78, 112–114
Tuschmid, August, 31, 37, 97
twin paradox, 78–80

U
Ulm, Germany, 21

W
World War I, 85, 86
World War II, 86–88, 92–95, 96

Z
Zionism, 86